Contents

GW00370644

This booklet draws upon the work of
Susan Williams of PPA's East Midlands Region.
We are grateful to Susan for her permission to use it

Drawings by Tony Benjamin
Cover photographed by Margaret Hanton in St. James Playgroup

Typeset by The Ikthos Studios
and printed in Great Britain by Caric Press, Andover, Hants SP10 1JE (0264) 354887

Starting Maths

For many adults, sadly, the idea of mathematics is associated with anxiety, confusion and failure.

For young children this is not so. Their experience of life is not divided up under subject headings and they encounter mathematical ideas and concepts as part of the whole enjoyable and fascinating process of finding out about and making sense of the rich, mysterious world they live in.

In maths as in everything else, children's understanding is based on personal experience and experiment. Children have to observe and explore the concrete world, using their senses, before they can deal with abstract ideas. They learn about space first of all by moving through it; about numbers by handling numbers of *things*; about variable quantity by seeing for example that their dinner is "all gone".

Mathematical learning is also built into learning about other things. Children playing at the sound table may discover that long chime bars consistently make deeper notes than short ones or that milk bottles with a little water in always make a higher note, when struck, than milk bottles with a lot of water in. When they do this children are learning about music, but they are extending their understanding of maths too. They will use that understanding later on when they learn to talk about proportions and ratios.

The children will clarify their basic understanding more readily if an adult is there to help them talk through their experiences.

This book aims to show how children can use their play activities to start building the network of mathematical ideas which will be extended and developed later on – in school and in their adult lives.

Children have individual experiences and interests and learn at different rates. But the way they learn follows similar patterns as they:

■ **explore** the world around – seeing, touching, doing, questioning;

■ **discover patterns** in what they see and do;

■ **repeat** actions and **test** the patterns they have recognised;

■ add their new **understanding** to what they already know about what the world is like and how it works;

■ use **words** to make clear what they know.

Conservation

When we say of a child, "She knows her numbers," what we often mean is that she can recite the *names* of numbers in ascending order. This is quite a useful thing to be able to do, but it means very little in itself. Children – and parrots – can repeat a list of numbers without having any understanding of what the words mean or how they relate to one another.

If children are to "get on" with maths later, it is very important that they come to know what the number system really means. They can be helped to do this through their play.

One of the first things they have to learn is about *conservation*: that three is always three, no matter how it is arranged or presented, whether it is **three, 3** or :., three bricks, three buttons on a coat or three Billy Goats Gruff.

Before a child can understand numbers for things that can't be seen – three claps, three miles, three years old – she needs real objects which can be seen and handled, with a chance to check that the count is right each time.

Children exploring this concept need a chance to look at the same number of objects in different ways. Some children, having been helped to count the marbles, beads or bits of Lego on a tray, will think that there must be more of them if they are transferred to a tall thin jar so that they reach up higher. *These children, even if they can say the names of numbers, have not yet understood about*

number. They need more opportunities to handle the materials and move them around until they begin to understand that the total number never changes unless some of the objects are taken away.

When they have reached this stage, children will not be misled into thinking that there are more ducks in the picture where they are spread out.

They will also understand that the jugful of dry sand, even though it may take different shapes if poured into different containers, will remain the same quantity and will fill the same jug again at the end if they do not spill any.

Play with clay and dough can make this concept clearer, as the same quantity of material can take many different *forms* while remaining the same *amount* and keeping the same *weight.*

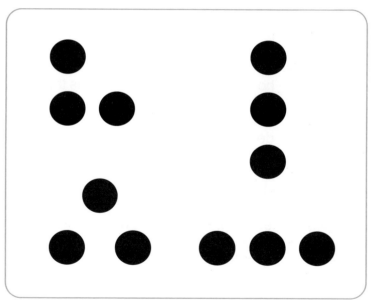

The same number can take different shapes

Correspondence

Counting involves knowing that each object counted must be matched with a single number. This is called *one to one correspondence*. Watch the child who moves a finger along a line of objects while reciting a string of numbers but without making them match. She has not yet understood about correspondence and needs more experience of one-to-one arrangements to get the concept clear.

Make-believe play offers many opportunities for this sort of learning. As the child builds a stable for each horse or gives a party for the dolls and teddies, setting a chair for each and giving each of them a place and a cup, she is gaining practical experience of correspondence. When she clears away at the end, if you have arranged it so that the number of cups in the home play area is the same as the number of hooks on the cupboard, she will be able to match one against the other and to use her developing understanding to check whether all the cups are there.

Similarly, when she buttons up shirts – for herself or a doll – she has to match each button to its buttonhole. (Even if she makes a mistake she is still learning, especially if an adult is there to help her see that *one* button left over at the bottom means *one* buttonhole left empty at the top.)

Snack time is anther occasion with a lot of mathematical potential. One to one correspondence is clear to see when you give out "a biscuit for Darryl, a biscuit for Sita, a biscuit for Kelly" direct to each child. Later when you count a biscuit for each named child onto a plate, the children will find they have exactly the right number when they pass the plate round. Later still, you can just count the children without using names and match the number of biscuits.

If the children help with food preparation they can have lots of practice in putting one cherry on each biscuit, a spoonful of filling on each samosa or a tomato on each plate.

Putting equipment away – at the end of the session or after an activity – can also aid recognition of one to one correspondence if each box has its own marked place on the shelf or if the block in which the scissors are stored has just the right number of holes.

Some groups make use of children's developing understanding of this concept to "ration" the number of places at activities such as water play by putting out a limited number of aprons – one for each child – to keep the numbers constant.

Sequence and Counting

Counting means arranging numbers in order so that each is one greater than the previous one and one less than the one ahead. There are lots of ways of helping children to think in terms of *sequences* where things have to follow one another in order:

■ Provide graduated beakers for stacking; graduated measuring jugs for sand and water.

■ Let the children arrange pictures in the right sequence for telling a story.

Counting is easier and more interesting if you use real objects, especially if you have collected them together yourselves. Use collections of similar objects – conkers, acorns, corks, bottle-tops.

You can provide more structured counting games, when appropriate, by giving the child a box and asking her to put four cones in it; to match the number of pebbles you've placed in an identical box; to count out the number of shells shown on the box itself, or on pictures on a work card.

'Count-down' rhymes like *Five Currant Buns* and *Five Little Ducks* won't teach children the meaning of the numbers but will give useful practice in remembering their order. If you make some papier maché "buns" or let some children be "ducks", with one disappearing or sitting down at the end of each verse, children can be helped to understand how the numbers relate to real objects.

Shapes

Awareness of shape is important, both for maths and for language development. Children can recognise the outline drawing of a solid object, or its silhouette or shadow, by comparing shapes.

Encourage the child to use touch as well as sight to find out about shapes, especially if she has difficulty with seeing. Use feely boxes or bags where she has to rely on touch to identify the objects she can't see. First, talk with the child before hiding the objects about the shapes of the things she will be handling and how she will recognise them again. Later when she understands the game, this won't be necessary; challenge her with unexpected objects.

At a festival time, put out a pile of brightly-wrapped presents and invite the children to guess what's inside. Some children will enjoy helping wrap the presents and making someone else guess.

■ Collect items of identical shape but different size and texture for interest tables or collage.

■ Provide regular shapes in various materials, to be used for picture and pattern making.

■ Use items of one shape for printing – or offer different shapes and ask children to choose *round, square* or *triangular*.

■ Encourage recognising, matching and naming regular geometric shapes by using them on (bought or home-made) lotto, snapcards or dominoes. (Remember to include different types of triangle and rectangle.)

Sorting

Many mathematical ideas depend on *comparison,* knowing what is meant by *the same* and *different.* Things which are exactly the same can be *matched* with one another. Things which are different can be sorted into *sets.* A set is a group of things which have something in common.

All sorting and matching activities help children develop discrimination skills. The desire to sort and classify is often triggered off by having large quantities to examine. A big bag full of autumn leaves might encourage a child to sort them in lots of different ways:

- according to colour
- according to shape
- shiny and dull ones
- intact ones and damaged ones
- ones which smell nice and ones which don't.

Make-believe play often involves sorting objects into sets. Children in the home play area sort crockery from pans; red mugs from blue ones. Playing with the toy cars, they separate those whose doors will open from those with fixed doors; ones which can tow other vehicles from ones which can't. The dolls house presents the challenge of sorting according to function: furniture

for the bedroom has to be separated from equipment for the kitchen.

Children and their families can be involved in the set-making which is necessary in organising the playgroup:

- collecting for the interest table 'themed' items such as cubes, yellow things, round things, things which can be magnetised
- bringing in materials for the collage table and sorting them for use into (eg) big boxes, small boxes, shiny things, bottle caps
- helping to pack things away at the end of a session and sorting wooden blocks, plastic bricks, beads and cars into their appropriate containers

As children come to understand about sets, they can enjoy games which require them to spot the 'odd one out'.

Don't forget that there can be more than one "right" answer to exercises like this. If you ask children to pick out the odd one from pineapples, apricots, plums and parsnips, the answer you are expecting might be *parsnips because they are the only vegetable,* but you might just as well get the answer: *apricots because the others start with the same sound,* or even: *plums because I like all the others!*

Space

An important aspect of mathematics is being able to recognise and organise the position of objects within a particular space and in relation to one another.

Children's first experience of this mathematical concept comes through movement. As they change their own position in relation to other things they become aware that objects are three-dimensional, with spaces between them. Some children explore this idea by trying to fit themselves into little spaces; others expend a lot of energy rearranging objects within a space and rejoice in having large cardboard boxes to push about.

Children whose disabilities prevent free movement can miss out on these early mathematical experiences and may need adult help to be as mobile as possible.

Constructional materials are very useful for extending children's grasp of relationships in space. Children may use building blocks:

▪ to create an enclosed area

▪ to build high or wide structures

▪ to make symmetrical objects/buildings

▪ to create road/rail tracks which make connections between other objects.

The same ideas can be explored at the painting easel as children create outlines and fill them in, or find out how many blobs they can fit into that space in the corner of the painting.

As children move around without bumping into one another – on vehicles or perhaps in response to music – they increase their awareness of space and of moving objects within it.

Words are especially important if children are to fix in their minds the concepts built up through activity. Adults need to be alert to add an idea or a question or to invite children to talk through what they are doing at the right time, *without interrupting the play.*

Time

Very young children are not usually ready for learning to tell the time, but it is important for them to develop and clarify the *concept* of time.

Before they begin to look at systems for measuring blocks of time – hours and minutes, days of the week, months, dates, seasons, years, etc – children need a chance to build up some idea of what time is.

One way to recognise the passage of time is to look at the changes it brings. Children can be helped by:

- sprouting seeds/planting bulbs
- watching tadpoles
- having a visit from a new kitten, and subsequent visits as it grows
- looking at babies and remembering/being reminded of when they themselves were small
- seeing photographs of their parents/playleaders taken when they were younger

Record-keeping within the group also builds up a sense of time. Children and adults together might:

- keep a weather chart through the week and talk about the changes
- make plans for special events and record them afterwards by means of photographs, drawings/paintings and written accounts dictated by the children.
- make a birthday calendar or a loose-leaf book with a page for each month, a seasonal picture and the name and date of each child's birthday.

Estimating and Measuring

In the course of their play, provided they are given sufficient raw materials to explore, children encounter many kinds of measuring systems. They discover:

- **quantity** as they handle *numbers* of conkers, cars, pine cones, etc

- **volume** by dealing with materials such as sand, water, clay and dough

- **capacity** while pouring sand and water between containers which hold different amounts

- **weight** when they pick up lumps of clay or shovelfuls of damp sand

- **width** as they adjust the bridge they have made so that big cars can pass through

- **height** through their attempts to build towers and as they measure themselves against one another.

The use of comparison in this way – to describe things by comparing them with something else – is an important aspect of mathematics. Some of the measurement words which young children use most frequently, such as *big, long* and *small,* are relative terms. Children may need help in talking through what they mean by them so that they realise that a *small* elephant is a lot bigger than a *big* mouse.

They will also need an adult at hand as they experiment with clay, sand and water to help them put words to their experience of things which *hold more than* others, or are *less than, longer than* or *heavier than,* others.

Estimating

As they become more confident in their understanding of basic mathematical ideas, children will be able to make predictions about:

- *how much* flour they need to stop the dough being sticky

- *how many* building blocks they need to close the gap in the wall they are building

- *which* plant pot will be *big enough* to hold a bulb, or two bulbs

- *how many* spoonfuls of paint will give the paint mixture the colour and texture they want

- *how large* a piece of dough they need to make a head for the monster they are creating

- *how small* a cover they need for the bed of the tiniest doll.

Taking measurements

It is often easier for a young child to understand a real object (a handspan, a pencil, a yoghurt carton, a spoonful) than a conventional unit of measurement such as centimetres, litres and grammes. Experimenting with their own forms of measurement will strengthen children's understanding of measuring systems. They may need help initially to see that if you have decided to measure something in brick lengths, you need to keep to a single size of brick.

The children's grasp of measurement systems is assisted if the bricks they build with are based on a common unit so that they can perceive relationships between the various shapes and sizes.

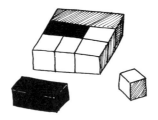

There are many activities in playgroup which children can enjoy while developing mathematical skills:

Using scales

Equal weights in a balance are easier to understand than dials or a set of weights. As they balance objects against one another children clarify their idea of *weight* and separate it from *size*. (They might initially be surprised to discover how many dry leaves or how much cottonwool it takes to balance quite a small piece of clay or a few marbles.)

Cooking

This activity provides one more example of *sequence* – things have to be done in a particular order; you can't add the water to the pastry until you have rubbed the fat into the flour – as well as encouraging children to use exact measurements in order to get the recipe right.

The ingredients might be measured in terms of weight (grammes/ounces) or volume (cup/spoonfuls) or liquid measure (litres) and the children can be helped to talk about these.

Height Charts

Lots of children have these at home and a termly measuring session in the group lets the children talk about time and growth as well as coming to terms with metres and centimetres. Other things can be measured in this way too: fix a plastic tape measure to the wall or fence behind a sunflower and see how it grows.

Bar Charts

Lots of people, children included, find mathematical ideas easier to understand if they are presented visually. Why not conduct a survey in the group? Find out who prefers apples/bananas/mangoes or who likes dogs/cats/hamsters best. (Looking at likes and dislikes is less competitive than asking who *owns* what.) Then arrange the information in columns to show the results.

Using Symbols

A number can be represented in various ways:

- By words, spoken or written
- By pictures
- By figures
- By numbers of marks – dots, etc.

These are all ways of expressing an idea by means of *symbols.* The power to understand and use abstract symbols is very important and it is based on experience with lots of concrete examples.

Some simple games for children are designed to help them clarify the use of symbols in this way. There are jigsaws in which the number 2 is divided into two pieces; 3 into three pieces and so on. (If you cut up old birthday cards you can make your own.) Some dominoes have the number represented by a figure at one end of the card; by a number of objects at the other end.

For children who have grasped the concept and enjoy practising a new skill, counting books, which represent numbers by a range of symbols, are fun. But a child who has not yet reached that level of confidence will learn more quickly by handling real objects and being encouraged to sort, weigh, arrange and count them until the idea of number becomes clear.

The Language of Maths

Words are no substitute for doing things. Children need real objects to touch and handle; actions to perform and repeat. But words *are* valuable tools when the child tries to put into order and explain what she has learned by doing things, or to make generalisations.

So although adults have to be careful to avoid lectures or intrusive chatter, they have much to offer in bringing the right words at the right time to the children's activities.

A good mathematical vocabulary, which is understood because it has been learned on the job in real situations, helps make the child's mathematical ideas clearer now and lays the foundation for future development.

Talk about:

Shapes – use geometric names where appropriate but encourage children to use their imaginations too; a child who calls a round shape *the sun* or *a ball* is recognising roundness as characteristic of them.

Sizes – contrasts (large/small), comparisons (bigger than, as tall as) and precise words (tall, narrow, long) which help children identify which dimension – height, width or length – is being described.

Sequences – not just *one, two, three,* but *first, next, last; first, second, third.*

Numbers have different names in different languages. Adults should be able to count with each child in the group in her or his mother tongue. (Learning to count in someone else's language can be fun too.) A child who has the opportunity to learn and practise mathematical vocabulary in her home language at the stage when concepts are being formed shouldn't find it difficult later to learn the English words.

Don't assume that just because a child uses a word she can understand the ideas behind it. Find out whether she can use the word accurately in other situations too.

Patterns

Recognising systems and sequences and the spatial relationships between things is an important part of mathematics.

Pattern-making is universal, occurring in music, language, and the natural world, but it takes different forms in different cultures.

Children may describe anything – from a quick scribble to a highly structured design with very deliberate choice and arrangement of colour and line – as a "pattern". We also use *pattern* to describe the irregular but distinctive markings on (e.g.) a tabby cat or tree bark. More precisely, patterns involve recognising, copying or creating formal arrangements of matched or linked shapes.

We can use children's pattern making to encourage discrimination and to introduce the idea of symmetry. As in other areas of children's play and learning we must be careful to match what we offer to each child's present understanding and skills. *Don't give too much, too complex or too soon.*

Draw children's attention to the patterns all around: on wallpaper, bricks and tiles, curtains, dress fabric and wrapping paper. Can they see how the pattern is repeated? Can they recognise and name spots, stripes, checks?

In their own art, children may deliberately set out to create a pattern or might recognise and develop one created by chance. This often takes the form of repeating a newly discovered shape: spots or rainbows or sometimes letters or figures.

Encourage both exploration and pattern making by offering material like mosaic tiles, gummed paper shapes, pegboards or geometrical shapes in felt or plastic to arrange freely. Later, children can use the same materials to repeat patterns you have made or to plan their own.

By folding paper you can create patterns built on symmetry. Paint on one half of the paper and fold it over to make a mirror image. Talk to the children before unfolding the paper about what they will see.

Fold and cut/tear paper to make doyleys or "snowflakes". Look at the pattern made when light shines through the holes.

As children become more experienced in pattern-making, you can fold and unfold a piece of paper so that the creases form a grid to guide repeating patterns.

Copy traditional patterns or create your own. Making a symmetrical design and sticking on coloured rice powder or sand creates Rangoli patterns.

Thread necklaces or festival garlands, asking children to copy a pattern or to create a repeating pattern.

Play with natural materials is useful for developing children's under-standing of repeated shapes. Let them make "reverse sandpies" by pressing a mould into sand, dough or clay to make an impression. If you make imprints in a slab of clay and leave it to harden, you can ask the children to find which shapes made which imprint. Limpet shells, bottle caps and buttons all make good impressions.

Encourage children to talk about:

- The changing patterns in a kaleidoscope

- The pattern water makes coming through a colander

- The repeated shapes and fabrics in a piece of patchwork

- Why you can't use a teapot to make sandpies.

Money

Most young children are taken shopping and many occasionally hand over money for a purchase themselves. Playgroups often go on shopping expeditions to buy ingredients for cooking or food for the hamster.

However, in the "simple" transaction of handing over money in return for goods there are complicated variables such as the value of currency and the pricing of some articles as units and others by weight. Many young children, having watched adults handing over money and receiving change, come to the conclusion that the kind shopkeeper hands out money as well as goods!

When children's makebelieve play includes playing at shops, we can make things simpler for very young ones who don't yet understand numbers by giving them large plastic or cardboard tokens, all of the same "value" so that the "customers" and "shopkeeper" can master first the principle of handing over one "penny" for one item and two "pennies" for two items.

Slightly older children can be encouraged to look at coins to sort them according to size, shape, colour, weight and finally value. They might enjoy making rubbings of coins, noticing the figures which show the value and the different pattern of heads and tails.

Later still, once they have understood that one coin is worth five or ten of another coin, some children may reach the stage of putting (e.g.) a 5p coin at one side of a balance drawn on a big piece of paper and counting out the right number of single pennies to go at the other side. (*You can't use a real balance for this because the value of coins is not directly related to their weight.*)

Games to Play

A lot of toys for young children are designed to develop mathematical skills:

■ *Recognising shapes and fitting them into/posting them through matching holes.* Developing and practising the physical skills helps to reinforce understanding, so children who have difficulty using eyes or hands need encouragement and access to toys which are easy to identify and to move. Simplify tasks for slow learners to help them master one stage at a time. (E.g. cover up all but one hole on the posting box and supply only one shape. Then go on to two.)

■ *Recognising sequence in items which are the same shape but graduated in size.* Ask the child to find a stacking beaker which is bigger than yours; or one which is much smaller; or the very smallest of the Russian dolls.

■ *Matching:* For younger children the interest and the fun, as well as the learning, lie in making the right match and completing a set, not in competing to finish first or score more points. A young member of the group might play better alone or with an adult, turning up all the picture cards and picking out the matching ones. Later you might find it useful to simplify bought games, such as Snap, by reducing the number of cards in the pack. You can make your own simplified lotto games using wrapping paper with repeating patterns, labels from tins/packets, catalogues, advertisements, or your own drawings photocopied.

■ *Combining numerals with other ideas:* Older children can count the spots on a die and use the information to play games such as the ones where you build up a beetle, house or dinosaur with numbered pieces.

PPA Guidelines –
Good practice for sessional playgroups
Good practice for parent and toddler playgroups
Good practice for full daycare playgroups

PPA Play Activities –
Glueing
Make believe play
Sand and water
Clay and dough

Learn through play –
Language through play

Starting a playgroup

What children learn in playgroup – A PPA guide to the curriculum

The business side of playgroups

The playgroup session – a guide for those who organise it

Accident prevention and first aid

A complete list of PPA publications and goods is available for SAE from: Pre-school Playgroups Association, 61-63 Kings Cross Road, London WC1X 9LL.